AUTH(

My name is Beth Caller, a self-proclaimed poet, and a bit of a dreamer. As someone who had a somewhat difficult start to life, poetry was an effective way to cope. I never really told anyone I would engage in the hobby, because it felt more like a distraction than anything else. However, when I saw how much poetry can help people like me, I decided I would have a go at authoring a book. I do not expect this book to reach too far. But if it can help one person, I am happy with that.

This book tells a story of my life growing up as a young woman in circumstances that may be considered quite unfortunate. Although, I want to note that I am grateful for who I am now, how far I have come, and the love I am surrounded by.

I did not want to have my work be completely depressing, so there is a bit of humour thrown in every now and then.

Dedicated to my family and friends for getting me through the tough times.

VIOLETS IN THE DARKNESS

Beth Caller

ISBN: 978-1-0369-0629-0

CONTENTS

GARDEN OF YOUTH

HIS FACADE

When I was a child,
A vampire lived in my home,
His eyes bloodshot and wild,
He would make us feel utterly alone.

He'd suck the life out of her,
And I would pick up the pieces,
My whole childhood became a blur,
A tiresome battle that never ceases.

We'd escape at about 2am,
Fleeing the hungry demon,
But she'd eventually fall back to the mayhem,
His hold on her defied reason.

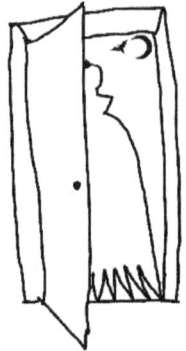

The monster would use his mind control,

To keep us in 'our place',

It's obvious he sold his soul,

We just had to roll over and brace.

We didn't share the same blood,

He had no right to our home,

Still he dragged us through the mud,

And our abode was his to own.

Sometimes I would hear his bellow,

And immediately flee,

Next the thud of something he'd throw,

My breathing hitches and tears flow as I
yearn to be free.

Sometimes I believe I'd have been less scared,

Had he truly been a vampire,

At least my sanity might have been spared,

And a little sunlight would set him on fire.

AUTHENTICITY: LIBERATION

Sometimes I felt like I had no real personality,
Adjusting to what others wanted to see,
I felt disconnected from reality,
So far from where I wanted to be.

I would shrink into the shadows,
Give someone else the spotlight,
Ignoring their sly blows,
I'd do anything to avoid a fight.

I liked living in my comfort zone,
No risk of embarrassment,
A little place to call my own,
Safe from harassment.

But eventually I exited my shell,

Realised what I was missing out on,

I began to treat myself well,

And the girl who wanted to fit in was gone.

When I started to treat myself right,

Beautiful individuals entered my life,

Being real showed me the light,

And sliced through negativity like a knife.

I know I have a unique personality,

And I don't care what others want to see,

I enjoy my own reality,

I'm exactly where I want to be.

SELF DEFENSE

Terrified child,

Trying to protect *her mum*,

Searching for comfort.

A CHILDISH HELL

I was just a child,

When I had the life drained from me,

I was just a child,

A child who would beg to be free.

I was just a child,

Whose light was overshadowed by the
darkness shown,

I was just a child,

Tormented by her peers' degrading tone.

I was just a child,

Who wanted to feel love,

I was just a child,

Consistently met with an emotional shove.

I was just a child,

Who would try her best to forget,

I was just a child,

Who could not forgive the pain inflicted yet.

I was just a child,

When I pulled myself out the rut,

I was just a child,

Who had to force the door shut.

I'm no longer that child,

And the monsters are gone,

I'm no longer that child,

Who learned too early to *just push on*.

I WONDER

I wonder what it's like,
To be born with money,
To be a spoilt little tyke,
Who thinks poverty is funny.

I wonder what it's like,
To not count your losses,
To always have the newest bike,
Unburdened by capitalist forces.

I wonder what it's like,
To not worry about your next meal,
To not have to strike,
To have time to heal.

I wonder what it's like,

To know daddy has it covered,

To be able to be childlike,

Instead of feeling smothered.

I wonder what it's like,

They wouldn't see the big deal,

Feign sympathy then laugh – 'SIKE!',

Despite the constant dread I feel.

I wonder what it's like,

I wonder what it's like...

FRAGMENTED HEART

Fragments of a little girl's heart are held in
these pages,

Please treat the pieces with care as you
progress through her ages.

-For that little girl

BUTTERFLY EFFECT

I want to go back,

Because I grew up too quickly,

Childlike wonder is something I lack,

As trauma was laid on thickly.

I want to go back,

Because I missed the naïve stage,

I constantly felt under attack,

Forced to act older than my age.

I want to go back,

And relive the happy parts,

Convince myself there's not much to unpack,

And what happened just improved my street smarts.

I want to go back,

And live a 'normal life',

I want to come back,

To an adulthood free of strife.

BREAKING THE CYCLE

I'd never let a teenager suffer like I did,

It's not that anyone was at fault,

But I was a terrified kid,

Bombarded by constant assault.

It was too much for a young girl to witness,

And despite lots of apologies,

It took a toll on my mental fitness,

Affecting my future ideologies.

So I continue to stand for what is right,

And involve myself if I must,

It will never be out of spite,

Only to do what is just.

Boundaries were always hard to set,

But I finally managed it,

Without experiencing regret,

I discovered where I fit.

I will always help others,

Because no one deserves my teenage fate,

I will always help others,

Because my help came too late.

FLOWERING CONNECTIONS

ARRIVING AT NEW DESTINATIONS

Romantic love no longer appeals to me much,

But I'd do anything for a cuddle from my best
friend,

I don't really care for lusts cruel touch,

When I adore my platonic soulmates to no
end.

Romance has an all too familiar sting,

But my family life my spirits every day,

You can keep your fancy diamond ring,

Those who love me will always stay.

Because romance is fleeting,

But my cat lays on my chest every night,

I've had enough of my energy depleting,

And the love that already surrounds me fills
me with might.

Why would I need romance?

When I provide myself with the love I deserve.

I'd rather not take the chance,

And focus on developing my self-worth.

I'm surrounded by beautiful souls,

Who make me feel easy to adore,

Romance won't keep me from my goals,

And I won't settle anymore.

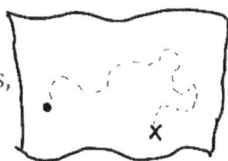

Romance no longer appeals to me much,

Because I've improved my aspirations,

I've escaped romance's clutch,

And I'm arriving at new destinations.

FAMILIAL COMFORT

Some families are strained,

But mine is always by my side,

Their love was never feigned,

And they always did their best to provide.

My family have held me through my darkest times,

While my life fell apart,

They helped to inspire my rhymes,

And stitched up my broken heart.

-For all my loving grandparents

PARENTAL SACRIFICE

My parents have been broken,
But they always stood by me,
With soft words spoken,
They provided me with the strength to be.

They cast their pain away,
To show me they were proud,
To make me who I am today,
So I could stand out from the crowd.

-For Mum and Dad

MY MOTHER

I never wanted to be like my mother,
Because I wanted life to be easy,
She was forced to change for another,
And what she experienced makes me queasy.

I never wanted to fight like she did,
Or do it on my own,
Ever since I was a kid,
I've witnessed her feel so alone.

I never wanted to cry myself to sleep,
Or despise the person I became,
I always held her and let her weep,
Praying I never endure the same.

I never wanted to be angry at this existence,

But rage was forced upon me,

Due to humanities evil insistence,

That altered the world I see.

I never wanted to be like my mother,

But when I witnessed her pain,

I realised this world's cruelty can smother,

And I may never be the same again.

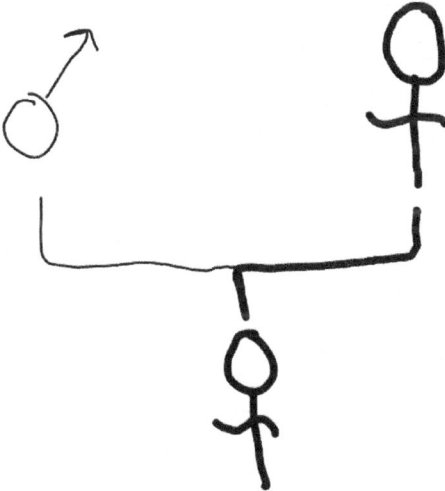

DEVOUT SUN

Your friendship is like a breath of fresh air,
How you instill me with your wisdom on cue,
Showing me how you care,
By teaching me things I never knew.

Your absence would leave me blue,
You are my sun which I cannot live without,
This type of love is completely new,
And my heart is totally devout.

-For Shaan Kaur

UNSEEN COMFORT

Some nights are spent staring at my ceiling,
Just praying that you're proud of me,
It's a bittersweet feeling,
Something I may sense but never see.

It's not something we often ponder,
When a loved one is still here,
But now I often wonder,
Whether I inspire those I hold dear.

I've learned to cherish every day,
And try my hardest to succeed,
To always communicate what I must say,
And to help those in need.

These are truths I already knew,
But never acknowledged enough,
Until we lost you,

A life cut short can be so tough.

Your life was so fulfilling and full of love,

You never failed to make us smile,

I strive to do the same - so you look from above,

And see me doing something worthwhile.

Life can be extremely short,

So now I live every day for the ones I hold dear,

To make them proud and offer support,

Because there's not enough days in a year.

So some nights are spent gazing at my ceiling,

Knowing you are proud of me,

I'm comforted by this feeling,

As it's something I sense but may never see.

-For Grandad Colin

A HEALING COMPANION

Some friends enter your life,
To heal parts of you they never broke,
To free you from some kind of strife,
To force you forward with a playful poke.

You are that friend,
That got me through it all,
When I could not see light at the end,
You never let me fall.

-For Jodie

LOVES MEANING

Love keeps me moving,

Love inspires me to do more,

Love gives us meaning.

THORNS OF HEARTACHE

FINALLY FREE

I've been trying to escape,

But you're only concerned with your own joy,

Driven by your selfish needs,

Manipulating me like a mere toy.

You decided my purpose is to serve,

Where the fuck did you get the nerve?

But I want to scream... I try to plead,

Your ego is no longer something I wish to feed.

I've always been whole without you,

Happier on my own,

I've been trying to escape,

However you demand I don't leave you alone.

A narcissist won't care how I feel,

How could I be so naïve?

You treated me like I didn't exist,

So our relationship... I finally leave.

I've managed to escape,

Yet you still won't allow me to rest,

You were always the one who needed me,

And I was just *trying my best*.

UNSEEN WORTH

I don't like who I am through your eyes,

Just another participation prize,

To earn respect from your guys,

Based on my curves and size,

You won me over with desperate tries,

Yet I was only fed more lies,

Disregarding my desperate cries,

While another piece of my heart dies.

A HEARTS TENDER REVIVAL

You call my name,

My hands begin to shake,

Although you're not to blame,

I define you as a mistake.

You reach for me,

I turn away,

Despite your plea,

My heart is not something you can easily
sway.

I tell you to leave,

I've been burned before,

I'm aware your aim is to deceive,

And that's not something I'll willingly endure.

But I can't avoid you forever,

Love isn't something to escape,

Yet I remain on my endeavour,

My image of love stays bent out of shape.

However sometimes I find myself reaching back,

Remembering that little girl with big dreams.

Before the world willed my heart black,

And before love had to suffer my unyielding schemes.

It's at times like these,

That my hesitance ceases,

I feel my cold heart unfreeze,

And I begin to pick up the pieces.

I take a walk outside,

And see a world so beautiful,

I set aside my pride,

And discover my heart is transmutable.

On my journey I find two beautiful tabby cats,

Cuddling outside a coffee shop,

With nothing to keep them warm but little pats,

And the love they shared that forced me to stop.

I turn around when I hear a mother and daughter sigh,

With nothing but admiration in their eyes,

The girl offers her last sweet to a homeless man nearby,

He sheds a tear as his spirits rise.

If love can be so inspiring,

Why must I despise it endlessly,

It's beauty I spend hours admiring,

So why do I avoid it so *desperately*?

BEYOND SURFACE-LEVEL

I don't have time for dating,

I don't mean I'm too busy,

I mean the process is excruciating,

And the only person I yearn to love is me.

Because frankly I don't care what your
favourite colour is,

And no I don't want another fucking drink,

I'm not trying to be a priss,

I'm just aware of how you think.

I'm not one for half-assed conversations,

Or beating around the bush,

Don't give me those baseless assumptions,

Ones on my character which you often push.

You don't know who I am,

And you never will,

Because neither of us really give a damn,

And I hate how you make me feel.

I am not what you see,

You don't know my story,

Nor do you understand me,

Frankly your attempts are corny.

I'd prefer to focus on myself,

I have accomplished so much,

Let's leave distractions on the shelf,

You can look but never touch.

You ask what my favourite colour is,

I tell you it's grey,

Obviously, I'm taking the piss,

But this conversation is purposeless - and I'd really like you to go away.

EXPOSURE THERAPY

I used to fear being cheated on,

The mere thought would torment me,

Terrified of a relationship built on a con,

I could never think clearly.

I've always had trust issues you know,

This was never a new feeling,

They didn't affect you though,

Because I had already started healing.

But you liked to test my boundaries,

Claimed I was unreasonable,

And would ignore my desperate pleas,

Because you knew your actions were
irredeemable.

I quickly found I was never the cruel one,

And you tried to destroy my inner work,

But darling I've only just begun,

How quickly I moved on makes me smirk.

I took time to reflect,

Upon what it was we lacked,

I could only happen upon your lack of respect,

And self-doubt was immediately sacked.

It's insanity really,

How this situation stopped my fear in its tracks,

I began to see more clearly,

And fill in all the cracks.

I walked away with my head held high,

Realising you're not worth my time,

There's no use in living a lie,

And the peace I found was sublime.

I no longer fear disloyalty,

Because those who love you never stray,

And if they can treat you with such cruelty,

They were never the one for you anyway.

IMPERFECT LOVER

I've been healing   my tainted heart,

But this would never   prove a painless task,

To request my lasting pain to agree to depart,

Can't be demanded and is too much to ask.

The pain is all my cold heart has known,

And I have tirelessly tried to heal,

The affliction has only grown,

And true love is not real.

If someone will care.

I'll get there.

Maybe.

EMOTIONAL REVIVAL

I was sure I could no longer feel,
Repulsed by the idea of love,
It no longer seemed a big deal,
I would push it away with a shove.

I walked away from feelings,
They only caused suffering,
Uninterested in romantic dealings,
Apparently my heart was just buffering.

Because in they walk,
With their constellation eyes,
Attempting to pick my hearts locks,
I scream and plead at their tries.

I want to run,

But their touch has me frozen,

My head told me I was done,

But now my heart has chosen.

I was sure I could no longer feel,

But my heart found another route,

I was sure I could no longer feel,

But with them - my screaming thoughts are mute.

A SERENE PRESENCE

My thoughts tend to race,
It can get a little out of hand,
I can't keep a steady pace,
Until your presence helps me land.

My thoughts will echo,
Until I'm in your arms,
You will them to slow,
With your calming charms.

I'm gasping for air,
Until you smile my way,
I can only stare,
And the pain slides away.

I'll be chewing on my nails,

Before you sweep me off my feet,

And with small exhales,

The fear begins to retreat.

My thoughts tend to race,

But not around you,

The peace of your embrace,

Is something completely new.

SHIFTING THE BALANCE

I will always comfort you first,
Even though I'm falling apart,
Whilst I'm at my worst,
With a terrible ache in my heart.

I will always comfort you first,
And you will gladly accept,
But my happiness is coerced,
As my boundaries are overstepped.

I will always comfort you first,
Then you'll walk away,
Leaving me feeling cursed,
Wondering why they never stay.

I will always comfort you first,

But sometimes I need help too,

I often feel as if I will burst,

As I focus entirely on you.

I would always comfort you first,

But that's not the case anymore,

Your empathy was always rehearsed,

And my head is no longer at war.

IVY OF AMBITION

PRESSURE IN PERFECTION

I should be doing more,

A thought I am often haunted by,

With my mind I am at war,

Despite how hard I try.

I should be doing more,

My head will scream,

Whilst my body is pressed to the floor,

And tranquility is but a dream.

I should be doing more,

But I already reached my peak,

My body and mind aching and sore,

I will not stop until I am weak.

I should be doing more,

But maybe I need a little rest,

I feel the tears pour,

From the pressure of a never-ending quest.

I should be doing more,

But I'm slipping into a dream state,

And as I feel the guilt roar,

I succumb to the peace that arrives too late.

MUNDANE STRAIN

Life can be so mundane,

Doing the same thing every day,

I beg to be freed from the pain,

Of knowing no other way.

I've been tempted to run,

But I have nowhere to go,

I feel I could follow the sun,

Away from a life that leaves me so low.

The days start repeating,

And the light starts fading,

Stuck in the same old seating,

It's my happiness I am trading.

I don't know how to break the rotation,

Without leaving myself lacking,

I do the same as the rest of my nation,

So why do I feel that I am slacking?

One day life won't be so mundane,

And maybe I can change my every day,

Until then I can take the pain,

Knowing I will find *another way*.

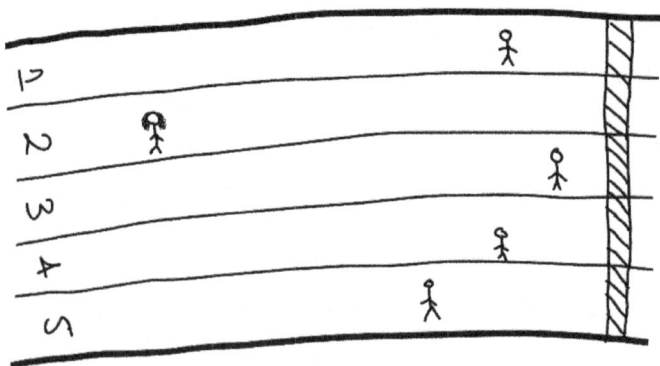

ENDLESS EXHAUSTION

No matter how much sleep I get,
I am always tired,
I can't decipher the cause yet,
And I feel constantly wired.

I walk around in a daze,
Trying to make some sense,
And hoping it's just a phase,
The exhausted feelings frequence.

I feel my eyes closing,
Begging for relief,
I become close to dozing,
The pull is beyond belief.

But I've got so much to do,

I must stay awake,

My energetic moments are few,

And I'd really love a break.

It might not seem too bad,

But this feeling will ruin my day,

It drives me half mad,

Until I reach my bed and lay.

AN UNCERTAIN SELF

I am confused by my identity,
It changes by the day,
I'm an uncertain entity,
Just trying to find my way.

I'm unsure of my direction,
And life seems mundane,
If I try engaging in reflection,
It may drive me insane.

I feel as if I haven't done much,
Although I'm told otherwise,
I begin to feel out of touch,
Because I can't believe the 'lies'.

But tomorrow I'll feel gifted,

Like I've achieved a lot,

My energy would have shifted,

And I'm ready to take my shot.

Things change quickly for me,

And it can be scary,

I never know how I'll be,

As my days tend to vary.

TECHNOLOGICAL CORRUPTION

Social media is poison,

With unrealistic expectations,

Social media is poison,

Built on evil foundations.

Social media is poison,

Which has rewritten the definition of love,

Social media is poison,

One I am not above.

Social media is poison,

And it draws us in,

Social media is poison,

It eats at you until you're sickly thin.

Social media is poison,

It corrupts our brains,

Social media is poison,

And keeps our children in chains.

Social media is poison,

I've always been easy prey,

Social media is poison,

And on it I shall waste away.

BEHIND THE MASK

'I'm tired' I say,

Even though it is not what I mean,

'I've had a long day',

It has been this way since I was thirteen.

A façade I have been moulding,

Whilst I am totally exhausted,

I can feel my sanity unfolding,

And reality is distorted.

Every day is a fight,

One I am yet to win,

I hope to soon see the light,

So I can let someone in.

Even when I rest,

I am not at ease,

Life feels like a constant test,

And my thoughts only tease.

One day I will shine,

For all to see,

One day I'll be fine,

To just be me.

FOREVER SHATTERED

Self-validation,

I have endlessly strived for,

But I keep searching.

X 10 Magnification Glass

WILTED VINES

OBSESSIONS UNYEILDING GRIP

My mind is a battlefield,

My attempt to confront obsessions is
incessant,

Yet they never seem to yield,

And my efforts are evanescent.

OCD is not just cleaning,

It's envisioning everyone you love *gone*,

It's compulsive repetition with little meaning,

At least to those who can just push on.

It's being late for everything,

While you're stuck in a loop,

Paranoia surrounding your actions - a
constant ring,

As if trapped in your own dreary coop.

For years I went undiagnosed,

Confused about my own mind,

I thought I hated myself most,

But some were truly unkind.

I recall one comment clearly,

'She's in fairyland again',

A phrase that was meant sincerely,

One that enhanced the lasting pain.

There are some things I still don't
understand,

A rare phenomenon I am yet to comprehend,

How – when it's bad – I lose control of my
words and actions that land,

As if my little power reaches its end.

I have coping mechanisms now,

I keep my head held high,

But for years I didn't know how,

And with my sadness I would lie.

DEPRESSIONS CLUTCH

I stay with him because he's all I know,

I stay with him because he comforts me,

Although my mood remains inevitably low,

I feel no desire to be free.

From young – he is all I've known,

He makes me feel less alone,

He keeps me in my place – in my zone,

'You're worthless' he speaks in a degrading tone.

He holds me captive in my bed all day,

And fills my heart with seething rage,

But it's a price I must pay,

To appreciate the words drafted on this page,

And for everything I was forced to endure at a young age.

His name is depression,

I would never let a person treat me this way,

I would never suffer this oppression,

Yet with him I lay.

Medicine temporarily numbs the pain,

But he and I are a pair,

True comfort is something I am yet to obtain,

As for my solace – he ceases to care,

Whilst I sit – quietly – *gasping for air.*

AWAKENING CLIMB

I lost a lot of time in my bed,

Trying to exit my head,

Filled with dread,

Until I fled.

In my prime,

I wasted my time,

So I began the climb,

Then I started to rhyme.

UNBALANCED RESCUE

I'll save you,

I tell him,

When I need saving too,

And reality remains dim.

I'll save you,

Whilst I sit and weep,

My mood still anxious and blue,

As I beg for a little sleep.

I'll save you,

Knowing I can't save myself,

Aware help is long overdue,

Disregarding my declining mental health.

I'll save you,

Ignoring my own screams,

You engulf my tunneled view,

And reality is lost to my dreams.

I'll save you,

I told you,

But I eventually withdrew,

Because no one would ever save me too.

FIGHT, FLIGHT OR FREEZE

Fight, flight or freeze,

I can never choose the right one,

As I feel my legs stiffen and my chest wheeze,

I notice I've lost the ability to run.

Fight, flight or freeze,

I can never respond correctly,

As I feel my actions seize,

I silently beg for someone to protect me.

Fight, flight or freeze,

A situation I've experienced too many times,

And as I buckle at the knees,

All that's left is my rhymes.

Fight, flight or freeze,

It's been the same option for a while,

Someone nearby will tease,

As I stare at the same floor tile.

Fight, flight or freeze,

I think I've given in,

I might never be at ease,

Until earth ceases to spin.

A BROKEN PATTERN

'Hurt people, hurt people',
Something I'm always told,
But I only ever take the fall,
Never allowing myself to be cold.

Hurt people have hurt me,
And I try to empathise,
But how can I allow this to be,
When I've been told so many lies.

I am a hurt person,
Who could never do the same,
Because the pain would only worsen,
As I'd struggle to pass the blame.

I've tried to heal those hurting,

Which has proven a mistake.

Their patterns were disconcerting,

And their own to break.

Now I'm a hurt person healing,

And I'm sick of it,

Forced to address this unpleasant feeling,

Because I endured too much bullshit.

BLOSSOMS OF RESTORATION

HEARTFELT EVOLUTION

I've been practicing self-love,

It's not always easy,

Sometimes I see the powerful woman who
rose above,

As often as the insecure girl I used to be.

The one who would do anything to fit in,

And still fail,

The one who hated her own skin,

A girl so melancholy and frail.

She would strive to understand the world,

Her social development stunted by childhood,

Societal demands were hurled,

She'd fall back and abide if she could.

No one knew the real her,

She didn't even know herself,

Surrounded by hurt and anger,

Causing deterioration of her mental health.

She was so ridiculous,

Couldn't she see how amazing she was?

She didn't need to fit in,

Maybe she would have been treated better
had she just been...us.

She was always kindhearted,

Always had the potential for self-love,

Maybe if someone had helped her get started,

It wouldn't have taken so long... been so
tough.

Yet here she is now,

She'll always be a part of me,

And even though she never knew how,

She taught me so much and I'll always love
her wholeheartedly.

I've been practicing self-love,

But I don't really need to,

I'm so proud of the woman who rose above,

And to that insecure young girl... I believe in you.

HELPING HAND

A friend's helping hand,
Allowed me to take a stand,
Her love was so grand.

A friend's helping hand,
Gave me a safe place to land,
To form the life planned.

TRANSFORMATIVE PRESENCE

You taught me to believe in myself,
And helped me to face my fears,
To look after my health,
And how to dry my own tears.

Some people can change you,
But in the best way,
You helped to heal me - I hope I did too,
I have no doubt you will always stay.

-For Megan

PROGRESSING WITH PEACE

'You're worthless',

My thoughts scream,

It hurts I confess,

But these words aren't quite what they seem.

These are not original thoughts of my own,

They can be attributed to those who brought
me down,

And made me feel completely alone,

The ones who tried to steal my crown.

To those people – I don't blame you,

It must have been entertaining,

I'm sure others would join in too,

Wouldn't bother abstaining.

I don't blame you – you were young and
naïve,

I'd scream that they were all rumours and
fakes,

But we were kids and easy to deceive,

I *have* made some small mistakes.

But nothing compared to what you had to say,

I just wanted to feel loved and accepted,

Yet that was a battle every day,

I suppose that's to be expected.

I had a beautiful heart,

And it was taken and twisted,

I suppose it was my fault for the most part,

Back then my boundaries never existed.

I became irrevocably insecure for a time,

And did anything to be liked more,

At least I have something to inspire this rhyme,

And teach me to be the friend I needed before.

The only way forward is forgiveness and love,

So I forgive those who made my teenage
years so rough,

But most of all I offer young me a dove,

For not managing to be a little more tough.

I'm much happier now,

I treat myself unbelievably better,

And I'm stronger somehow,

But I promise *I'll never forget her.*

PAIN TO FREEDOM

Healing   feels like

  a large   arrow

    to   the

      heart,

      If,

      you

      want

      to

      move

      on,

  You must grimace

   through pain

    and let

     go.

RECLAMATION

I've taken my body back,

More than once,

I've taken my body back,

A result of their carnivorous hunts.

I was so young,

I vow to protect myself now,

But it doesn't bring back the innocence to which I clung,

I wish someone would show me how.

I have walls up now,

Ones unlikely to fall,

But that's something I will happily allow,

To avoid what I'm forced to recall.

If you've never been in this position,

I will not heed your opinion,

I won't endure your falsified rendition,

From another patriarchal minion.

'Boys will be boys' they say,

Power to be abused from an early age,

But it's your daughters that pay,

And find it hard to turn the page.

These feelings of violation repeat,

But I've taken my body back,

I'll not be silent and take a back seat,

Since *I've taken my body back.*

SUNFLOWERS OF SELF-KNOWLEDGE

FINDING PEACE

I became tired of being silent,

So I decided to raise my voice,

Some may see it as defiant,

Those who love me rejoice.

I became tired of stagnancy,

So I decided to keep moving,

Those close support me,

And my mental health's been improving.

I became tired of the rage,

So I let it go,

I broke out of the cage,

I forgave and felt the anger slow.

But I became tired of forgiveness,

Found it hard to put things on the shelf,

You can't fix others sickness,

So I decided to mend and forgive myself.

So when it becomes hard to raise my voice,

When it's difficult to keep it moving,

I made self-forgiveness my choice,

Even when society is disapproving.

PAINLESS PRIDE

I always wanted to make everyone proud,
But there was only one person that mattered,
I always wanted to make everyone proud,
But I ended up completely shattered.

I always wanted to make everyone proud,
And I managed to do just that,
I always wanted to make everyone proud,
Then discovered I'm happy where I'm at.

SUCCESS' SHADOW

Everything has been going right,

But my chest will still tighten,

I can finally see the light,

Yet my world doesn't brighten.

I've been working on myself,

Although my cheeks remain stained,

Maybe I should focus on my health,

Rather than the social expectations I finally attained.

I thought those achievements would make me happy,

Maybe I'd finally feel at ease,

But I'm still feeling pretty crappy,

As I shake and fall to my knees.

I thought I'd done what I had to,

To make everybody proud,

But I burned out and split in two,

Using my success as a shroud.

I've become accustomed to the chaos in my mind,

I'm tormented by my own thoughts every day,

Peace isn't something I easily find,

As my uncertainty begs to stay.

So I will begin to focus on balance,

Rather than pleading ignorance.

I will utilize my genuine talents,

Maybe then I will see a difference.

KEY TO GROWTH

You are always there to support me,

And scold me if you must,

Your love is my key,

And you have never betrayed my trust.

Some friends feel like home,

They have the perfect tools to comfort you,

Providing you with the strength to roam,

Towards a life that is fresh and new.

-For Megs, Matt, and Dan

FULL CIRCLE

Life can have its challenges,

But everything will come full circle,

The healing process eventually begins,

Allowing everything to come full circle,

However - much like this uneven poem,

The healing process is not perfect,

But it all comes full circle.

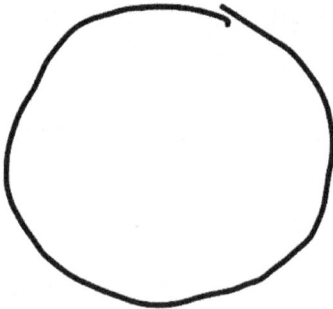

TOGETHER WE HEAL

I will always support a woman in need,

No matter how many times she goes back,

I will always help to plant a seed,

Until she is ready to pack.

I've seen the woman closest to me lose her self-worth,

Pick out every one of her hairs,

Because of a man too wicked for earth,

But I will always fix her tears.

I would do the same for a man,

But that's not the focus of my rhyme,

Because too many women are dying... *again... and again...*

At the hands of a man's horrific crime.

Domestic abuse laws exist for a reason,

And for them I'll forever be grateful,

But women lost their lives for legislation,

We live in a world so cruel and hateful.

So a woman can go back a hundred times over,

It doesn't matter to me,

I will still support her,

Until the day she is free.

SELF-FULFILLED SMILE

I spent time working,

I smiled as *I made it*,

And held my head high.

FULL BLOOM

I think I'm finally finding my way,

And little me would be so proud,

I used to fight every day,

Now I stand out from the crowd.

A person who shows true care,

And acknowledges the trivial things,

An individual so undoubtedly rare,

Who indulges in the beauty nature brings.

You'll hear true happiness in her cackle,

And join her as her eyes light up,

Knowing challenges are something you can
both tackle,

As she compliments you and fills your cup.

This woman is kind,

She will make you laugh,

She has a brilliant mind,

Someone who will always give you half.

She is who I have been searching for,

And I'm so glad I found her,

I've become someone who I adore,

And I'm so proud of who we were.

ACKNOWLEGEMENTS

To my Nanny Val, you provided me with the courage I needed to finally work on this book, I am forever grateful.

To my Nanny Sylv, you have been encouraging my inner poet since one of my first poems was published in year 9. You have always believed in me and that means everything to me.

To my parents, you have always served as an inspiration to me, it goes without saying that a part of your love is held in these pages.

Thank you to my best friend, Shaan Kaur, who provided me with her beautiful illustrations (she knows I am notoriously bad at drawing).

Made in United States
North Haven, CT
24 January 2025